GREEK SACRED SITES

ATHENS
THE ACROPOLIS

JILL DUDLEY

PUT IT IN YOUR POCKET SERIES
ORPINGTON PUBLISHERS

Published by
Orpington Publishers

Cover design and origination by
Creeds, Bridport, Dorset
01308 423411

Printed and bound in the UK by
Creeds

© Jill Dudley 2016

ISBN: 978-0-9935378-2-0

ATHENS

THE ACROPOLIS

The goddess Athena was the patron goddess of Athens, and her temple was the Parthenon. The Parthenon, as we see it today, despite all the wars and vicissitudes experienced by it, still stands supreme in all its ancient majesty, dominating the Acropolis at the heart of Athens.

In antiquity the goddess Athena was popularly known as Athena Parthenos (Virgin Athena). Her birth was a strange one. Her father Zeus, supreme god of the ancient world, loved Metis, a wise Titaness whose name means 'thought, counsel'. Zeus was told, however, that any son of Metis would become stronger than himself so, to avoid any chance of that, he swallowed her. Some time later he developed an excruciating headache and implored Hephaestus, god of fire and metalwork, to split open his head with an axe. This he did and Athena sprang mature and fully armed from his head.

Athena was the embodiment of wisdom and the owl was associated with her; she was often depicted with an owl perched on her hand. She was goddess of war and victory, hence her epithet Athena Nike (Nike meaning 'victory'). A small and elegant Ionic temple c.420 B.C., dedicated to Athena Nike, stands on the south-west corner of the Acropolis where the rock is at its most precipitous. It is allegedly from this point, with its view to the sea, that King Aegeus, father of Theseus, kept watch for his son's safe return from Crete* where he had gone to kill the Minotaur. They had agreed before he left that if successful, Theseus would hoist a white sail on his return, if not, there would be a black sail. Sadly, Theseus forgot this pre-arranged signal and his father, seeing a black sail, was so distraught he cast himself off the Acropolis to his death.

Athena was also goddess of handicraft, especially spinning and weaving, and was protectress of many cities, hence the appellation Athena Polias (of the city); but in particular she was patron goddess of Athens. Before Athens came under her protection, though, it is thought to have been ruled by a mythical king named Cecrops. Rather oddly he was thought to have been shaped as a man but with a serpent's tail – a sort of son of the earth, the snake symbolizing the forces of the earth. In those days snakes were not considered evil, but were symbolic of divine wisdom, and Athena was often seen accompanied by snakes as well as the owl.

It was during this reign of King Cecrops that it is said a quarrel developed between Athena and Poseidon, god of the sea; they were arguing over which of them should have power over the city. The gods decided that each should present a gift, and whichever was thought to be the most beneficial would be given the city. Poseidon struck the rock in the vicinity of today's Erechtheion, where they say the mark of his trident can still be seen, and from it came a spring of salt water representing sea and trade. Athena, on the other hand, presented the city with an olive tree which offered food, oil, wood and, above all, peace. The gods awarded her the city which then took her name, hence Athens.

In antiquity on the Acropolis the Athenians believed that an olive-wood image of the goddess which they possessed had fallen from the sky. It depicted Athena seated and holding a bowl in her right hand. An annual ritual was held when the people dressed this image in a *peplos* (a woollen cloth pinned at the shoulders and draped over the body), which they hung with ornaments. Every year these were removed and the wooden image was taken down to the sea for purification.

This earlier festival was thought to have been initiated by King Erechtheus and was called the Athenaia in honour of the goddess. As early as 700 B.C. a small temple was built, close to where today's Erechtheion is, in order to house the ancient wooden image. The temple was destroyed by the Persians in 480 B.C. together with Athena's olive tree; miraculously, though, the old tree put out a new shoot and grew again; there is still an olive tree growing there today, a descendant of the original. The olive tree represents all that is good: food and prosperity, the olive branch of peace, hope and resurrection. During the reign of Theseus (who had become king after his father had cast himself off the Acropolis to his death), he reorganized the scattered communities in Attica and turned them into city-states, whereupon the festival was renamed the Panathenaia.

Gradually over the years the Panathenaia developed from being a simple procession and sacrifice to the goddess, to a much larger celebration. Athletic and equestrian contests became part of the festival. What was known as the Lesser Panathenaia was held annually, and the Greater Panathenaia every four years on the 28th day of the month of

Hecatombaeon (roughly July/August), said to be the birthday of Athena. Musical contests were later added also. The winners of these various events were awarded *amphorae* (large jars) containing olive-oil from Athena's sacred olive tree.

On the final day of the Greater Panathenaia the festival ended with a magnificent procession which was a continuation of the ancient tradition of bringing a newly woven *peplos,* the new robe for Athena, to her statue. The procession set off at sunrise led by young girls selected from the most prominent families. There were basket-bearers carrying the implements for the great sacrifice, others bringing sacrificial cakes, water-carriers, old men bearing olive branches, officials, envoys, musicians, hoplites (infantrymen), as well as men on horses, and chariots, together with the the many sacrificial animals.

Athena's first temple in which the wooden image was housed was located south of, but close by, today's elegant Erechtheion on the north edge of the Acropolis. At that time there was a King Erichthonius, semi-divine, who often assumed the shape of a serpent (continuing the earlier King Cecrops serpent tradition). Erichthonius acted as custodian of Athena's old temple in which he also lived. The ancient olive-wood image of Athena was kept to the east of this building and, according to the second century A.D. travel-writer Pausanias, a gold oil-lamp burned continuously there, needing refilling only once a year.

Today's Erechtheion is impressive with its elegant proportions in the Ionic style, and its Caryatid maidens supporting its southern porch, was built in the latter part of the fifth century B.C.

It was at this time, when the renowned statesman Pericles

was in power, that the *Propylaea* (the great entranceway to the Acropolis) and the Parthenon as we know it today were constructed. It was the combined work of the architects Phidias, Callicrates and Ictinus. Phidias, however, was not only an architect but also a talented sculptor, and it was he who was responsible for the sculptured marble frieze, metopes and pediments on the Parthenon which were the envy of the world. He was also responsible for the twelve metres tall gold and ivory cult statue of Athena which would have stood within this new temple. Phidias' cult statue of Athena was dedicated to her in 438 B.C. at the Panathenaia festival. It was this festival that was depicted on the marble frieze by Phidias, and ran around all four sides of the temple (160 metres long). On the metopes (sculptured panels) were scenes from the great battles of the past, including the siege of Troy in which Athena had played a major part in supporting the Greeks with her divine intervention. The east pediment sculptures depicted the birth of Athena, while on the west was the contest between Athena and Poseidon.

To the east of the Parthenon is a very ancient sanctuary of Zeus where wheat and barley were sacrificed on his altar. There was a very strange but ancient tradition: an ox was allowed to approach and eat these votive offerings, a priest then killed it with an axe, which he immediately flung away, after which he fled. Subsequently, charges were brought against the axe which was banished from the city, or cast into the sea. This was the oldest known ceremony – even in the fifth century B.C. it was considered extremely ancient, and was thought to have been instituted by King Erichthonius. It might well have been associated with the birth of Athena who was born to Zeus when his head was split open with an axe.

An estimated figure of twenty-two thousand tons of Pentelic marble was quarried from nearby Mount Pentelikon for the construction of the Parthenon. Today it stands majestically, dominating the city's skyline, despite being denuded of its exquisite marble sculptures which are now in the British Museum.

The only justification for Lord Elgin removing the 'marbles' is that, if he had not taken them for England, then the French would certainly have had them. Lord Elgin, however, suffered for it, as though the twelve Olympian gods were taking their revenge. The first calamity was when the ship carrying them foundered off the coast of Greece and the 'marbles' had to be salvaged from the sea-bed at great expense. Next, Elgin's wife left him taking her fortune with her; one of his sons died, and another had epilepsy; finally, Elgin himself suffered from an unfortunate disease which disfigured his nose and his career prospects were ruined.

It is interesting that St. Paul when he came to Athens must have set eyes on the Parthenon when it was at its most magnificent with all its sculptured marble frieze, metopes and pediments. He preached to the Athenians from the nearby Areopagus, a small rocky elevation a few metres from the Acropolis on its north-west side. It was there that those accused of blasphemy had been tried. St. Paul had been brought there for being a 'babbler' and preaching 'foreign divinities'. Apparently the Athenians were totally bewildered by what St. Paul was preaching. They treated him very politely: '...and they took hold of him and brought him to the

Areopagus, saying, "May we know what this new teaching is which you present? For you bring some strange things to our ears; we wish to know therefore what these things mean.'" (Acts 17:19) St. Paul's visit resulted in two converts, one being Dionysios the Areopagite. It is interesting that the name Dionysios containing the 'i' at the end denoted a devotee of the god Dionysos, god of wine and drama.

When Christianity was finally imposed by the Emperor Theodosius II in the fifth century A.D., the question was what to do with the Parthenon, this unique pagan landmark in the centre of Athens which was the heart and soul of its citizens. Rather than destroy this ancient and magnificent monument, it was decided to convert it to a Christian church. By modifying its interior and making an entrance at its west end, and building an apse to the east which was originally the entrance to the Parthenon, it became the city's cathedral. From being the temple of Athena, the embodiment of wisdom, it was first dedicated to Agia Sophia (Holy Wisdom), then later it became the Church of Parthenos Maria (Parthenos meaning 'virgin'). From the worship of the virgin goddess Athena came the worship of the Virgin Mary. By these subtle means the worship of Athena was eased out gently.

In place of the ancient mid-summer Panathenaia festival held in honour of the virgin goddess Athena, in the fifth century the Emperor Mauricius introduced a major Christian mid-summer festival held on the 15th August in honour of the Virgin Mary. It remains one of the greatest days in the Greek Orthodox Church calendar.

In 1458 the Turks conquered the city, and the pagan

Parthenon which had been converted to a Christian cathedral became a mosque. But how odd it is that this great monument – what remains of it – still stands in all its marble splendour with its great fluted columns, and people still come from all over the world to admire it.

Instead of only seven wonders of the world, surely the Parthenon should be counted as the eighth and the greatest?

* Denotes a separate booklet on the subject.

GODDESS ATHENA'S FAMILY TREE

Chaos
— Gaea
— Ouranos
— Metis *m. Zeus*
(thought, counsel)
— Athena
(born from the head of Zeus)

GLOSSARY OF GODS AND GODDESSES

ATHENA – Daughter of Zeus and Metis. She was goddess of victory, weaving and handicraft, and also protectress of many cities, but especially of Athens. She was the embodiment of wisdom, and in the classical era her symbol was the owl.

DIONYSOS – God of wine and drama. He was the son of Zeus and the mortal woman Semele. Zeus' wife Hera was enraged by this extra-marital affair, and persuaded Semele to ask Zeus to show himself to her in his full glory. This he did which reduced poor Semele to a cinder, whereupon Zeus rescued his unborn son and placed him in his thigh from which in due course Dionysos was born.

HADES – Brother of Zeus and Hera. He was god of the underworld.

HEPHAESTUS – Lame son of Zeus and Hera. He excelled in metalwork and made exquisite artefacts in gold and silver.

HERA – Wife and sister of Zeus. She was goddess of women and marriage.

KRONOS – A Titan. He was married to Rhea who gave birth to many of the Olympian gods, including Poseidon, Hera and Zeus.

METIS – Consort of Zeus. Her name means 'thought', 'counsel'. Because Zeus was told any child of hers would be more powerful than him, he swallowed her, and in due course gave birth to Athena from his head.

POSEIDON – God of the sea and earthquakes. He was brother of Hera and Zeus.

RHEA – A Titaness, and wife of Kronos. She was mother of Poseidon, Hera, Zeus and other Olympian gods.

TITANS – The offspring of Ouranos (often spelt Uranus, the heavens) and Gaea (the earth). There were said to be twelve of them, six sons and six daughters. Kronos was one of the sons, and Rhea one of the daughters. These two gave birth to Poseidon, Hera, Zeus, and several other of the Olympian gods.

ZEUS – Son of Kronos and Rhea. He was supreme god of the ancient world once he had deposed his father. He was god of the heavens, the giver of law, and dispenser of justice. He was married to Hera but had many extra-marital affairs with mortal women.

MORE FROM THE
PUT IT IN YOUR POCKET SERIES
GREEK MYTHS

TROJAN WAR
THE JUDGEMENT OF PARIS
HELEN
KING AGAMEMNON
ACHILLES
THE WOODEN HORSE
ODYSSEUS

ISLANDS
CHIOS – HOMER
CRETE – THESEUS AND THE MINOTAUR
KOS – HIPPOCRATES AND ASCLEPIUS
NAXOS – THESEUS AND ARIADNE
RHODES – THE COLOSSUS
SANTORINI – THE LOST ISLAND OF ATLANTIS

ALSO BY JILL DUDLEY

YE GODS! (TRAVELS IN GREECE)
YE GODS! II (MORE TRAVELS IN GREECE)
LAP OF THE GODS (TRAVELS IN CRETE
AND THE AEGEAN ISLANDS)